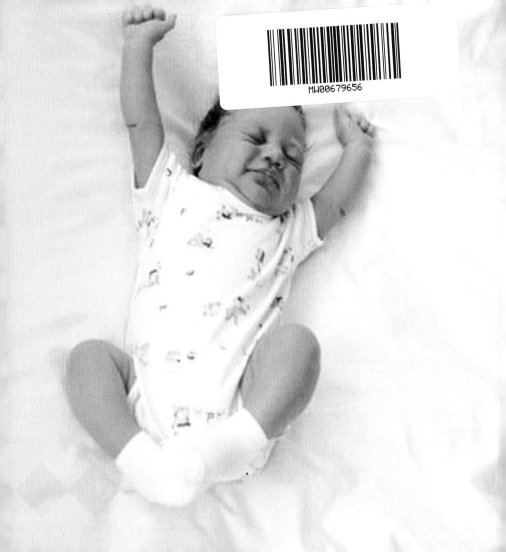

MW00679656

Every desirable and beneficial gift comes out of heaven.
The gifts are rivers of light cascading down from
the Father of Light.

James 1:17 THE MESSAGE

Presented to

Presented by

Date

Where did you come from, *baby* dear?

Out of the *everywhere* and into here.

George MacDonald

It's a
BOY

Celebrating the Arrival of Your Newborn

my sweet boy

We can't form our *children*

on our own concepts;

we must take them and *love* them

as God gives them to us.

Johann Wolfgang von Goethe

Children are a gift from the LORD;
they are a reward from him.

Psalm 127:3 NLT

You have set your *glory*

above the heavens.

From the *lips* of children and infants

you have ordained *praise*.

Psalm 8:1–2 NIV

People who say they

sleep like a baby

usually don't have one.

[God] will never let me stumble, slip or fall. For he is always watching, never sleeping.

Psalm 121:3–4 TLB

God's ways are as hard to discern
as the pathways of the *wind*,
and as mysterious as a tiny
baby being formed in a
mother's womb.

Ecclesiastes 11:5 NLT

A world without *children* is a world without ***newness***, regeneration, *color*, and vigor.

James Dobson

my sweet boy

Rock-a-bye, baby,

mommy's wee tot.

When the *moon* glows,

the cradle will rock.

'Til the dawn breaks,

may *Light* from above

Shine down upon baby,

cradled in love.

Kathryn Knight

A *boy* is the only thing

God can use

to make a *man*.

E. C. McKenzie

A good man obtains favor from the LORD.

Proverbs 12:2 NKJV

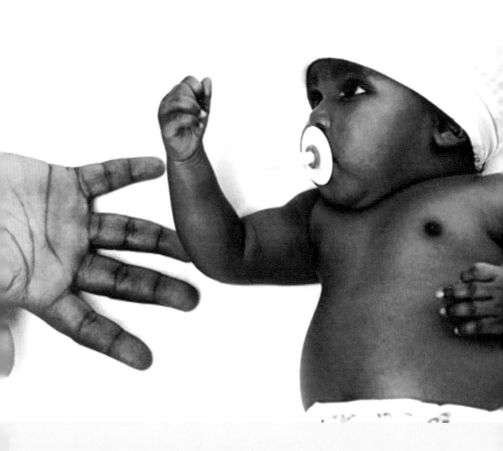

When you look at a baby, it's just that: a body you can look at and touch. But the person who takes shape within is formed by something you can't see and touch—the Spirit—and becomes a living spirit.

John 3:6 THE MESSAGE

The first time you lay eyes on your *baby,* you realize that God reserves a very special portion of your *heart* for him alone.

Sheila Booth

Beloved, if God so loved us,
we also ought to love one another.

1 John 4:11 NKJV

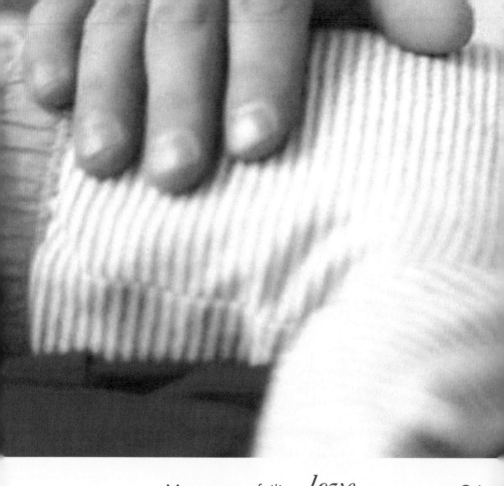

May your unfailing *love* rest upon us, O Lo

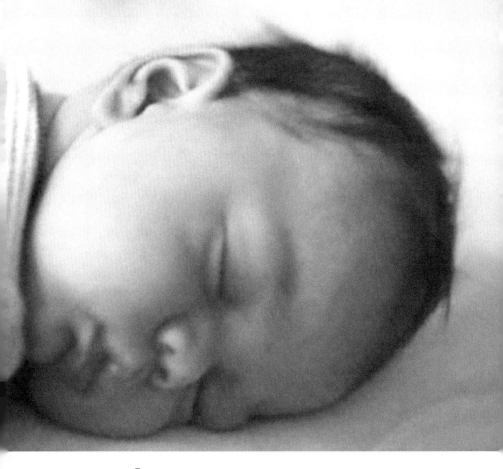

en as we put our *hope* in you.   Psalm 33:22 NIV

Hush! my dear, lie still and slumber,

Holy angels guard thy bed!

Heavenly blessings without number

Gently falling on thy head.

Isaac Watts

my sweet boy

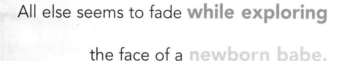

All else seems to fade **while exploring**

the face of a newborn babe.

Vivian Kelly

Oh, give thanks to the LORD,
for He is good!

Psalm 118:29 NKJV

Build me a son, O Lord,

who will be strong enough

to know when he is weak,

and brave enough to face

himself when he is afraid,

one who will be proud and

unbending in honest defeat,

and humble and gentle

in victory.

Douglas MacArthur

Boys will be **boys.**   Anthony Hope

He shall give His angels charge over you, to keep you in all your ways.

Psalm 91:11 NKJV

my sweet boy

Even a *child* is known by his deeds.　Proverbs 20:11 NKJV

Do not exasperate your
children; instead, bring
them up in the training and
instruction of the Lord.

Ephesians 6:4 NIV

Infancy conforms to nobody;

all **conform to** it.

Ralph Waldo Emerson

Jesus said, "Let the little children come to me, and do not hinder them, for the kingdom of *heaven* belongs to such as these."

Matthew 19:14 NIV

A **babe** in a house

    is a well-spring of pleasure,

        a messenger of peace and love,

    a resting place for innocence on earth,

        a link between **angels**

    and **men.**

Martin Farquhar Tupper

If **children** grew up

according to early indications,

we should have nothing but **geniuses.**

Johann Wolfgang von Goethe

Children's children are a
crown to the aged.

Proverbs 17:6 NIV

my sweet boy

He smiles, and sleeps!—sleep on

And smile, thou little, young inheritor

Of a world scarce less young:

      sleep on and smile!

Thine are the hours and days

      when both are cheering

And innocent!

Lord Byron

It takes **three** to make a **child.**

E. E. Cummings

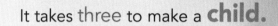

Thank you for making me so
wonderfully complex! Your workmanship
is marvelous—and how well I know it.

Psalm 139:14 NLT

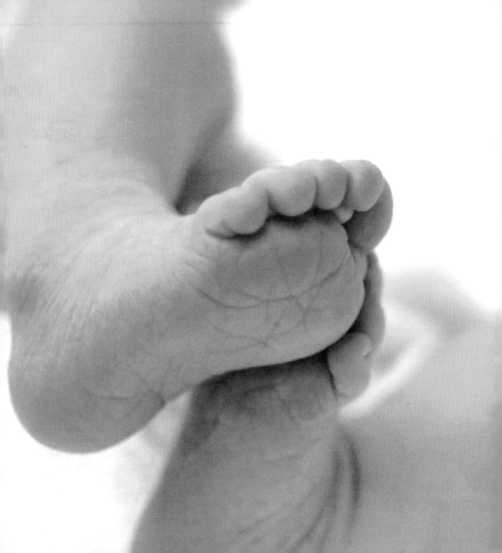

May the LORD give you increase
more and more,
you and your *children*.
May you be blessed by the LORD,
who made *heaven* and earth.

Psalm 115:14–15 NKJV

You made all the delicate, inner parts of my body
and knit me together in my mother's womb.

Psalm 139:13 NLT

The *heart* of a child is the
most *precious of* God's creation.

Joseph Whitten

Before I was born
the LORD called me;
from my birth he has
made mention of my name.

Isaiah 49:1 NIV

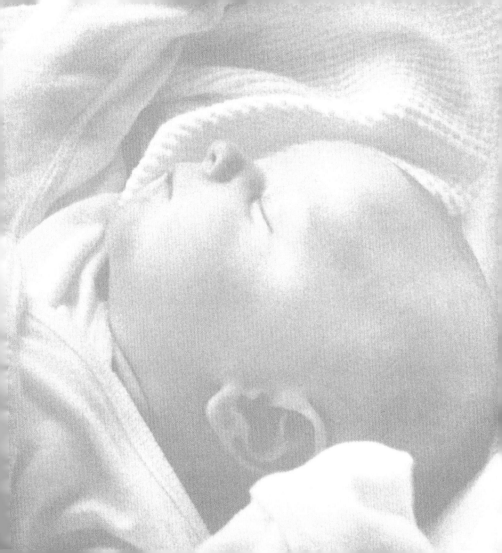

You don't raise *heroes*;
you raise sons. And if
you treat them like
sons, they'll turn out
to be heroes, even if it's
just in your own eyes.

Walter Schirra Sr.

He who begets a wise child will delight in him.
Let your father and your mother be glad,
and let her who bore you rejoice.

Proverbs 23:24–25 NKJV

A father *expects* his son to be

as good as he meant to be.

E. C. McKenzie

Sweetest little fellow, everybody knows;

Don't know what to call him

but he's mighty like a rose!

Looking at his mommy with eyes so shiny blue,

Makes you think that heaven

is coming close to you.

Frank L. Stanton

It's a Boy
ISBN 1-40372-025-8

Published in 2006 by Spirit Press, an imprint of Dalmatian Press, LLC.
Copyright © 2006 Dalmatian Press, LLC. Franklin, Tennessee 37067.

Editor: Lila Empson
Compiler: Snapdragon Editorial Group, Inc., Tulsa, Oklahoma
Design: Diane Whisner, Tulsa, Oklahoma

Printed in China

06 07 08 09 LPU 10 9 8 7 6 5 4 3 2 1

14944